New York City Rain

NARRATIVE POETRY

BY

D.J. ANDERSEN

"this is our kingdom of days..."

Bruce Springsteen
" Working on a Dream"
Columbia Records
Copyright Bruce Springsteen 2009

ISBN **978-0692352434**

© Copyright D. J. Andersen 2015
All Rights Reserved

IN MEMORY OF MY BROTHER

TIMOTHY JOHN ILG

Thanks to Jean, Lorraine and Steve.

You all helped make this book possible.

Thanks to Julie Ainslie, who left a message.

Table of Contents

LAUNDRY 1

ALWAYS LOVED 5

SNOW IN THE BLUE ROOM 7

ART, WHEN IT LOVED ME 9

MY FIRST TATTOO 13

CAUSE OF DEATH 21

HOW PRAYERS ARE ANSWERED 27

NEW YORK CITY RAIN 29

ON YOUR BIRTHDAY 35

THE DAY BEFORE ANNIE TURNED 30 39

JONATHAN'S DOG II 43

SHOWERS OF GLORY 45

THE RED HOUSE 49

WHAT LAND OF GLORY? 53

THE OTHER WOMAN 57

NICK 61

ART ON THE WALL 65

CHRISTMAS 67

THE SOCIOPATH 69

DEATH OF THE WIFE BEATER 71

RED LIGHT 73

LAUNDRY

she sits on the green- white couch with the

phone's receiver in her hand in case it might ring at least she can hear it.

she can't see the clock now, her eyes are shot, she

asks me five minutes after I've told her, what time is it? I

resist the sudden urge to say some time that it is not, same thing when

she asks what day it is, or if I brought her coffee, or if she took her pills,

but no matter what I say, she'll believe me for a minute, then forget.

so I take the too small basket overwhelmed with laundry down the wood white

steps to the basement, she is not supposed to one-step down here, everyone is scared

she'll fall and crack her head, lay in a heap til the next day or night.

I think she comes down here anyway,

in remembrance of defiance.

I tried to keep this basement white, I

painted it over and over all those years with the cheap gloss latex she insisted on. I kept on telling her latex wouldn't last on brick, she didn't care, she

thought, as usual, I didn't know what I was talking about, I don't think she

ever believed anything I said in all those forty years,

way before she lost the strength to keep her mind inside her head,

at least intact,

god.

she used to be intimidating.

dominating,

always craving something sweet.

but not that summer day

she

yelled at me when the cat mother brought her kittens under the front porch to keep them safe.

she screamed at me to get them out of there like it was my fault the cat loved her kittens.

she

walked in the side door and all through the house, out the front door,

I heard it slam,

then stomped like a rolling thunder down

the sidewalk to scream at me again to get the kittens out

of there right now. I stood on the grey porch—I painted that, too—

battleship grey, do you hear me?

wondered what she wanted me to do at the same time I was stunned.

you can't be screaming that loud

about anything in a neighborhood

at six in the morning they'll cart you off on a gurney.

when her screams turned to shrieks I called the police, to

shut her up.

they came with the dog warden, took the kittens and the mother cat,

stuffed them into crates, I hid behind my apartment door to see

if she'd blow out from the house and scream at them too,

two times.

soap first, then soiled, stained clothing into the washer with cold water—she insisted on that, too.

cold water!!!!

I didn't ever want to go upstairs again, if only I could climb out the broken basement window,

she ordered me to tape it up, she wouldn't get it fixed. I stood still and smoked two

cigarettes instead. she called out to me, wanted to know where I was, I thought I'd

say on the roof at the Holiday Inn,

but she wouldn't think that was as funny as I did. I stepped

all the way back up the stairs, it began to seem like miles,

so she could see me, where she asked so helplessly, earnestly,

if I had brought her coffee what day was it? what time was

it? and did she take her pills? and would I mind doing the laundry? and

would I remember to wash it in cold water? and please and thank you.

ALWAYS LOVED

kiss me.

before the sun sets in the distant west with sighs,

and I will love with what is love,

in that pitch of darkest night as it creeps along with longing.

hold me.

and I will lay my head upon the burdens of your shoulders,

inhaling all your aches and all your angers,

I need your necessary heartbeat in my hands,

for I have always loved and always loved.

touch me.

before the dawn comes to it's always eventual eastern rise,

never ceasing it's relentless effort to warm me.

it will be your kiss that halts my descent into sun steamed ash.

gently,

say no words that might be wasted,

we fall in one form upon the sheets of an unmade bed.

find me.

I am in pieces.

starved for sacrifices you have always offered me,

I reach back for them and anything insanely or innately good,

trying not to shatter everything and everyone I touch.

cover me.

I have rust in both my eyes

from years of crying into caverns I filled up with rivers, damming everything,

always knowing I have wasted you, shoved you in another room

with fires and fever and the winds of all my madness.

relinquish me

as the moon rejects the universe and sends it into spin and havoc.

this is the only moment that matters in a lifetime,

for I have always loved and always loved.

SNOW IN THE BLUE ROOM

can you fall with grace ?

can you fall holding onto

the pain of knowing you did the one right thing

for all the emotionally wrong reasons?

I'm here in the blue room

pacing back and forth like a fate maddening wind- up toy

drinking all the vodka from this bottle I bought from Phyllis for four dollars,

and I need to answer that question,

I need to know if it's red or it's green,

is it one adorned with thorns

and why it has to cost so much

to do the one right thing?

look at the wreckage.

The carnage on the floor of what was joy just yesterday

as I sat on the bed at six in the morning,

I will always remember that and I'll stare holes into this darkness and I'll set fire to that white memory over there.

at the liquor store I thought I'd pay for grace,

but it was snowing so hard outside I knew I'd answered my own question.

there were so many other ways to fall.

ART, WHEN IT LOVED ME

when art loved me,

I surrendered to it's sweet seduction

and loved so fiercely back, at times I could not find a breath.

freed from a stifling other truth I'd always been so bound by,

(that art is this and not that)

I fell into its open arms as if it were a lover,

listened to lullabies art sang low and softly to me.

a melody I might have known once,

when I was small and spoke with scribbling crayons,

my mother sitting with me on the white tiled kitchen floor,

where we drew purple lines and wiggly bluebirds,

drew silly forms and giggled,

 painted colors with our gooey fingers.

a time retrieved from a happier past,

I remembered it and

took the treasures back,

held them in my hands,

art had loved me then.

I had forgotten

how very happy just one line could be,

how bold and endless,

broken or sad,

carried even off the paper by my hand-made bamboo pen,

or brushed away on a gesso- washed canvas by my soft bristled brush,

lines fat

lines fine

lines old

lines limping

lines thin

lines faint as whispers only I could hear.

when it loved me,

art blew boundaries of shape away from me,

asked me

look again.

the angular, spectacular, heartbroken, delirious, magical.

hold hands with form.

the fantastic, fierce, forbidden, mindless and free.

hesitant, at first, to hold the hands of anything,

I wept at all the infinite that I could make them be,

the dark the day the night the new the heavenly haphazard

poetry of possibility that never needed rhyme.

when art loved me,

we danced to the music of color,

the crazy African Stomp of

yellows yelling for a place beyond, beside the out loud oranges

that ravished the reds whenever they could steal the moment,

the blues beyond my comprehension,

the whispering whites, lush lavenders.

beyond the glorious spectrum,

in the privacy of my own palette

I could mix the extraordinary everything.

when art loved me,

I understood the tenderness of barely brushed shadow,

it was a touch I treasured.

I beheld and held and the living light,

it fell on my shoulders as a sun screaming day in summer,

then it shimmered on the waves of a seascape

painted with my momentary hand.

when art loved me,

 saved me.

art paved a path to the everything endless,

where I emerged awed

 aware

all the world spins on art's axis.

MY FIRST TATTOO

I thought I heard the doctor say "cancer", but I

could not be sure, and I was not alarmed, his voice was far away.

I was deep in daydreams, scenarios of evil action for someone who I barely knew,

then,

sitting on the dining room floor, phone in one hand, I thought I

saw Christ in a porcelain bathtub, his holy water warmed with bubbles,

blue washcloth in his hand.

"We need to schedule **SURGERY!**"

I petted the kitten, I considered,

told him

NO.

I

can't.

there's no time for cancer, if that is what you said,

I have plans.

I got this AMTRAK ticket,

it's green on both sides,

I'm going back to The Big Easy.

"YOU CANNOT PUT THIS OFF!"

his urgency dropped from the phone and stood on the floor and faced me.

I stared it down.

In New Orleans

I'll seek a voodoo priestess.

she will mix a spell,

arrange a ritual,

likely one involving chicken heads and alligator eyes.

and as the headless chickens walk their headless walk around the cauldron,

I'll be blessed by dancing,

chanting I won't understand, but

being blessed in any language is being blessed just the same and I will

DRINK

the cauldron's brew from a careless mug or a piece of old stone jug.

the thick hot drink of spell will boil that malignancy away,

we'll lay back on bayou grasses, singing slow songs of the earth and fires,

pass around a hit of this, a drink of that.

I wrote **7:30 a.m.** under Tuesday on the calendar,

wished to know why my body had not slapped me with a red alert

the moment the malignancy had started—some drum banging monkey

in a red hat toy from my early childhood came to mind.

where were the sirens that should have screamed in my head?

I would have been crazy not to hear them

 and their CANCER warning running by on a screen somewhere right below my eyes

and underneath the headlines.

straight to HELL with cancer,

I'ma be on Bourbon street, baby,

stepping off the curb with a beer in my hand into a dancing crowd,

no more loony cells running around in me dragging cancer with them

in their foul and odorous madness.

I'm having a brunch at The Court of Two Sisters, I

cannot believe all this food and it's food I would expect to eat in heaven.

if I should ever want food again, it would be this food.

when I get out of this surgery and outta this fetid bed and out of this stupid tie-on gown,

I'ma run home and stay in the house, smoke up every cigarette that I can find or buy or steal.

Nancy would later tell me that smoking after having cancer was just bizarre,

she,

she said,

had quit her cigarettes so she

could be more healthy,

and I,

(remembering what Blanche would have said)

did not take off my hat to her,

just

offered out some weak congratulatory bits and pieces of bullshit,

and walked away to Ray's Place.

the night after surgery,

walking my IV pole around the room, I

hissed at a nurse in the darkness,

'where are they?

what did YOU do with them?"

possibly alarmed

she struggled for a word,

it was

"pathology."

purposely,

I moved in close enough to snatch her,

told her,

"FIND THEM!"

I would take them with me,

sit at home on the dining room floor

and glaze and fire them into ashtrays,

after I get back from this touristy store with handfuls of more

purple, gold, and green Mardi Gras beads.

CHEMO?

when piggybanks fly.

My Mardi Gras beads and these doubloons are better than chemo,

and in the early morning I love the smell of this river water,

it is sweeter than the smell off the docks in lower Manhattan,

and in this sweeter smell I walk out to cool my feet.

a needle full of pre-planned **POISON** jammed into the bulging biggest best blue vein

I ever had on my right arm was NOT the first **TATTOO** I got. I got it

at the small dark parlor across the street from our hotel,

it was a bright red rose bud with soft green leaves.

Tom covered his eyes at the sound of the gun,

while I studied the new sensation of vibration.

it wasn't that bad,

or if it was,

I'd never **TELL ANYONE** anything ever

about the pain.

or those two scars.

CAUSE OF DEATH

you're not dying very well are you?

there are no second chances handed out to get it right.

I've walked this tear and spit stained hall up and down and back and forth,

my hands jammed down into my jeans pockets, trying to remember

why I ever loved you.

I swept all the rooms of your great house before I

got here and I can finally breathe the air,

it's free of the sickening sucking sounds of your hospital stuff they surrounded you with.

I'm not letting Kim come in here,

she crashes into the ER carts with her riveted and sashaying thighs.

before Freda left this morning, I saw her with a grape

clutched in the fingers of one hand,

I watched her walking all around the big back yard,

Christ,

you'd think,

on a Tuesday, at least, she'd have kept better track of time.

Your expression hasn't changed for days,

your eyes are tightly closed and practically dead.

in the mornings they run in and out of your room so fast,

changing your sheets and your gown and your towels like

they got a reason to be in a hurry, they dart out and bunch into a ball

all the soiled sheets, along with blue and antiseptic rags and stuff

it all in a hanging canvas laundry bag.

I stared at you so fiercely that you bled.

I didn't care anymore,

it sure as hell beat nails into the day you reached your skinny arm out,

grabbed me, got my shirt stuck in your death yellow hand, demanded

I inform them that you wanted no more surgeries.

I don't care what you say.

Reba's down the hall now,

rocking their baby in her arms,

the baby blanket's corner hanging down like the tail of one bad dog.

You oughta get up.

walk right on outta here in fancy sling-back shoes and find your way into

your own account of heaven.

after all those years you flung it's promises up against the hell-fired bedroom wall,

well,

you oughta know the way.

when Sherry calls—and you and I know that she will—

she'll be sobbing again and cryin' for Jesus til God knows when,

banging her grocery cart off the concrete outside walls—

there's a cart, these days, for everything, it seems,

except

the life you wasted.

staring off into the Hill St. woods all those summer nights,

afraid there might be someone there.

there never was anyone there,

I told you over and over, yet

you

bolted the back door anyway,

didn't you?

one of those nights I said,

"Hell, let the criminals in!"

Now I'm just tired.

I'm through putting one foot in front of the other endlessly every goddamn yellow day

while you mutter and whisper in words you want us just to hear half of

behind all our backs,

could you ever give us just the satisfaction of knowing what you had to say?

your opinion of anything at all might have once mattered.

you move in your sleep,

you form a small sound.

it doesn't count now.

you grimace in what seems to be pain,

I've seen that look before a thousand times,

it's just the same as when relatives came to Sunday dinner,

they don't come anymore, and

you're not dying very well are you?

HOW PRAYERS ARE ANSWERED

gods take their places

while their fair-haired goddesses weep for some

reason neither they nor I are sure of.

everyone's prayers are held to be edited later on,

short ones first,

and I know this.

so I whisper to myself about the prayers I have hidden

and resolve to shorten them

so they'll be faster answered.

all the clouds the sky can hold bend down

with bad intent before they blow off to

some other place to wreak havoc,

and I know this.

I think something big is going to happen soon because when it

starts to rain,

it's not raindrops,

it's an angry and unholy madness that slaps the sides of my head

like the rains that Noah fled from in his ark.

I run inside to find my torn green rain suit, it's really cheap,

I paid for it at Walmart.

I don't really think it's going to save me,

but I gotta do something while I wait

for all the gods to find their places,

pick up everybody's prayers,

soothe the weeping goddesses.

I shortened all of them eventually,

took out all the words but

PLEASE and AMEN.

I hope these are the only words that matter.

NEW YORK CITY RAIN

the beer- bellied man brought my car down,

drove it out of the cage and threw me the keys.

I saw grease stains all over his yellow sweatshirt as he walked away,

he never said a New York word.

I seized the steering wheel with both my hands,

tried to ease it into traffic, but

they don't do it that way here,

in this city you gotta make a statement just to get in line.

so I make mine.

the cars in front of me inch up in increments—there's a

DETOUR

sign ahead.

I turn the radio on and out comes Springsteen's Mary,

she's dancing across the porch again,

the rain beats down,

it hammers dents on my car as the song about the old grey mare starts up from, well,

out of nowhere,

runs the verses I know,

stops,

repeats.

Lorraine, Diane and I linked arms and sang the song on one of these sidewalks,

moving people in a hurry always in a hurry, they had to walk around us, frowning.

this city roars

this city rises

this city never rests,

this city weeps like the black tears on my windshield,

this city doesn't apologize for anything,

this city rules the world.

you could come here with your dreams in a bag and do anything,

make it big here,

get a chance here,

be someone one day.

and some of them will,

and some of them do,

and some of them don't,

those are the ones who leave their sad and damaged dreams all

over these city streets and sidewalks,

I saw boneless forms of some yesterday, while walking.

there is an all full spectrum of colors here, in the night,

in the rain,

reds from the marquis, the traffic lights, the sirens, the signs for something everywhere,

some long and thin, some wider.

golds, yellows, whites from thousands and thousands of lights,

lights through windows and stores and small shops and bars, cafes and ethnic eateries,

Donnie and I ate at a Greek one, I had a macaroni block, a bowl of anchovies on the side,

one of the best meals I ever paid for.

In Ellen's Stardust Diner I paid for the worst meal I ever ate, I got pale and sick in the Marathon restroom, threw up bits of stuffing and cranberry sauce,

musical notes from 50's songs, I swore I'd never eat or listen to oldies again,

phone numbers, ads for sex acts all over the white stony walls,

why should I feel shame at the overflowing toilet?

there's a pointy purple ray piercing a billboard,

pinning some of the backlit lettering,

blues dive into the rain soaked boulevard, I saw

Zero Mostel in the Broadway play, "Fiddler On The Roof",

and then he died.

these ribbons of shimmering greens are the colors of the water slapping

the sides of the Staten Island Ferry,

that formed the edgeless shadows on the pond in Central Park.

there's a white Ford behind me,

the driver on his horn like it's my fault or something that we sit in a line of detoured traffic, as the yellow cabs in the opposite lanes speed, zip, fly, zig, zag by us,

as they have always done and they will always do.

When Tom was here, he said the city's too noisy,

the city's too fast, city's too hot (in August),

like there was something else he expected it to be,

yet

I understood.

it could be a week,

or maybe just eventually,

this city

overwhelms me, overheats me,

I'm in overdrive,

the energies here run through me like wires,

electroshock!

and I gotta shut it down,

I gotta stop the shouting.

the street cop waves me off to the right,

I'm on a street I don't recognize,

I'm in a momentary freeze,

I'm swimming in speeding thoughts of getting lost here,

there.

another

    DETOUR

sign to follow,

I'm okay.

I love it here,

there's a place in my heart for this city.

I switch from rock to a country music station,

it's Faith Hill, it's Blake Shelton,

it seems so out of place.

ON YOUR BIRTHDAY

if I could dart into dark tunnels I lost of the past, I

would do it

just once,

and only pull yesterday back,

leave all the others alone.

I'd have to shake yesterday out like a rug,

I know,

but

with it in my wretched grasp

I'd pull you close and clutch your hand and thank God for it.

my eternity was always etched out in your face,

I can't tell you,

I can't tell myself,

I can't tell anyone

why

I didn't know it

when I needed to know it

more than I needed to know anything else.

I love the red

of roses you sent me for Valentine's Day,

when I held on to your always startling laughter.

when I was blind for a day,

I laid all my possible futures

in one basket,

the one we bought in New Philadelphia.

they're now all the color of ash, and

I think you'd be amused

if you knew it.

I'm not at all stunned these days

at the shadows of age and weariness that have made themselves permanent

here

where I sit and stare out,

half crazy.

I might be

all the way out of my mind as I stare at the noise of a white summer day,

or at the long fields of gold grasses that wave at me constantly

even after I wave back.

didn't we swim in an ocean of awe?

didn't we run in the waves at Berlin?

we were drunk on the scotch from your birthday,

we had the time of our lives

til your wishes went down the drain as you showered

and mine in the kitchen sink as I washed plates and pots and silverware,

thinking that was what mattered.

where do you sit now and

what do you see?

I wonder if you'd ever want to

pull me close and clutch my hand and thank God for it.

this is the place I'll always be or come back to,

holding a glass full of scotch in my hand on your birthday.

THE DAY BEFORE ANNIE TURNED 30

this is the way she walks into waiting for miracles,

one foot at a time,

testing the waters,

her faith is tentative

when the water is **over** her head, she'll say she's been resurrected,

I don't agree, but stay silent.

shh.

say not a word.

she'll snap.

I've never seen anyone pace as much,

up and down and back and forth this long green hallway,

sorting through contradictions.

be careful, she warns me, her eyes filled with worry,

you can't hope for anything too much of the time.

in the morning she bathes in cold water,

throws her towel on the moon of circumstance to dry.

smokes and drinks her coffee black,

tells me sordid, SHOCKING things that move me to another room,

I lack the ribbon to wrap her present.

I DON"T WANT TO KNOW ABOUT THAT!

her laugh is mirthfully wicked.

on the front porch she sits in the high back wicker I painted white last year,

I've never seen anyone calmer.

emotions like clouds on a string fill her eyes,

sail away like a million kites.

she leafs through her book of promises,

says love is a delicate lace.

be careful,

she warns me.

there's hell to pay for believing in life in dreams and trying to make it all mean something.

there's hell to pay not to.

I agree, but stay silent.

SSH.

SHE"S BEEN BLACK AND BLUE BEFORE, I DON"T WANT TO WAKE HER UP.

the cake I baked drips chocolate frosting, it isn't big enough for 30 candles,

it's okay,

I've only got 29.

JONATHAN'S DOG II

The porch steps are cracked up, the ends of them crumble, no one we ever knew lives in this house any more, the porch swing was taken down long ago, folded up, the paint in that room was faded the last time I saw it.

I have not been here in years, and never meant to.

the bones of Jonathan's dog, red Labrador, are buried underneath these bushes that form a hedge around the yard, there is no dead dog ghost, but the smell of gas teeth is not broken as easily as the scent of promises that don't come true.

my hallucinations now do not include you.

I never try to find you now, I don't know where I'd look, and the certainty of your never being in my life again comforts me. back then, when every straw I held onto mattered, I flipped through all the pages in my life, I could not flip through yours.

I only truly loved you for one day.

In Montreal you sat outside the café, in a white metal chair, you sipped green tea from a fine china cup, green tea has so many health benefits, you said, as if you expected me to drink it, too. You wrote on the back of postcards, your handwriting so elegant and delicate, you told everyone that Montreal was peaceful, (and I thought, compared to what?), wrote that Canadians were friendlier, (than who?), you said you could live a life there, (but didn't). you licked the postage stamps yourself, stacked the cards up in a pile beside your napkin, waiting to send them off at just the right moment, you had to decide how you felt about things first, the postcards pictured with black cats with too long necks and over slanted green eyes, all your friends would get the same ones.

when the sun sat down on the breezy day, it trusted the unsteady hands of night, something I would never do, 'cause any love at all from you would be stilettos in my hands, my heart, and years before any kind of heat at all would melt them, and I would never have survived those deaths in 1982, it was the worst year I managed to crawl through, and those lesser woundings bled so bad I slipped into a three year coma. Nobody can lose that much blood.

I look up.

there, as I catch my breath, is the only thing we'll ever share in this lifetime,

this once again melon rind moon.

SHOWERS OF GLORY

you're cheap for a whore, he said.

I was diminished.

in a strangely hoarse voice not mine I said I didn't care.

I wanted my money,

he threw it down on the floor so I could bend my ass over, pick it up,

know my place and stay there.

he always calls, he can, and he knows it.

I'll always come, I must, and he knows it.

I'll do whatever he wants, and he knows it.

I'm cheap for a whore, and he knows it.

the motel charges by hour,

he pays at the drive-in window.

the bed sheets are grey and rumpled, wrinkled by the ones before us,

the carpet's stained, the walls are bare,

no frames to fall when he slams me up against the wall,

throwing open all the doors and windows.

my heart snapped shut so long ago I can't remember having one.

I'll be anything for anybody as long as I can have the money.

he's brutal, I'm bruised,

I watch him shave as I wipe the blood from my lips with a small and threadbare towel.

I'm gonna drink the money up,

I'm gonna drug the money down.

when I think about anything at all, I might hear my soul scream,

but that's all right with me, I never feel it,

'cause when the needle pops my vein I know

I'll see the face of God, I'll weep in showers of glory,

and what in this life could be better than that?

my God, dear God, the ecstasy of a sinner.

he said, you're cheap for a whore,

and I laughed out loud.

he rolled me over on the floor and

laid the money down.

THE RED HOUSE

the night the roof fell into the attic at the red house, I

hid behind a bedroom wall, I did not want to be drenched

by the raging thunderstorm. the lesbians upstairs sat around on red milk crates,

since furniture was not allowed, they screamed at each other, some were

adamant that only a female roofer would do. you should have seen their dining room

crates, stacked up high to make a table, crates placed lower to be the chairs, it cracked me, up they thought

they were so politically correct, I thought they were crazy, so I called Sam.

he found me a room in a yellow house,

it's roof was fine, it had no floor.

Sam said I don't know why you called me after what you did, this is

the best I could do, don't call me again, not even if you're fucking dying.

I tossed in limbo all night long, sorry I had called Sam, so grateful that he came to me at all after what I did, though the lack

of true and deep sleep left me weak and woke me to a dim

and startled morning. I crawled across the warped wood plank,

a make- shift bridge where holy water stank below, I

recoiled at the stench, surprised at the smell, did not have time to dwell on it.

later that day I made it all the way to the bus station, I don't

remember how I ever got there, and Deb said what the hell are you doing walking all over Cleveland in crutches?

dropped my coins on a slot, the fare for

finally getting out of there.

at home I changed my clothes and changed the bed.

needing music more than needing anything else, I hopped

to the downtown fest, a woman sang a song in German,

was it a song or was it rage on that way- too- well lighted makeshift stage?

I watched the notes drip off the edge of the floor

even before she finished, but the drummer kept beat in an odd, uneven silence.

I thought the whole thing odd, bewildered I pushed through the audience,

that thundered with applause, to the bar I played pool in,

the owner's mynah bird still screeching for an answer to the only one thing it could say,

"what's it to ya?"

incensed, I threw it to the sky, my anger fierce, I watched it fly, a

beer in my hand, I thought about faith, any faith at all, I

wondered why the gods and God kept tossing people in hells and fires

they said were far below, and why was fury so consuming needed when

maybe we could die in peace instead of on a spit and find a glory

in rooms without a floor and life without a thunder, life without tables made of crates,

life without crutches and life where trees did not fall in on top of roofs when storms grabbed hold of innocent lives and drenched them, and whenever a woman sang a song, her voice was strong and clear and even the lesbians in the red house would stop. and sit in awe at the prima-donna.

WHAT LAND OF GLORY?

it's miles of life I feel

in my head in my heart in my hands, I turn my palms up, I

cannot take another step in any direction.

I'm done.

I'm not.

I'm tired.

I'm caught.

I'm not even sure how I got here, aware I only stopped for water

and for weapons for wars always waged from a fear of something left to lose.

fiends with forces fanatic, enemies in ambush,

but it was my blood on my hands and not theirs,

and I'm not crying to Christ for anything, not

kneeling on my knees and praying with arms stretched out for

mercy where there isn't any left.

I got a taste in my mouth I'd like to spit out, if I did, nothing would change after all, so I roll my tongue around and swallow it down.

It's weight on my shoulders that's bending me into a hunch.

when I looked in the mirror this morning I had blood in my eyes. I'm

not even breathing, yet I find out often that I cannot catch my breath.

I passed love and your kisses by so long ago it's too late

to turn back.

there's thunder in the distance, a wind that blows my hair

around and away from my face,

I gotta get the dogs inside,

I need to close the windows,

I think I'll watch this new storm from the north

on my front porch in a careless, fearless way. I wonder

if I stood out there in the rain,

instead,

if I'd get rinsed and raised by these winds

to the land of glory.

(what land of glory? It's just a song, a poem, a story).

most likely not, I'd just get wet

and in wet clothes stay cold.

people say what people say when something said is needed.

"God never gives us more than we can bear."

"Don't wallow in self-pity."

"Everything happens for a reason."

"Time heals all wounds."

No,

it doesn't.

you just remember everything longer,

all your scars are wider and deeper and seem to take

forever to form and close.

and things happen because things happen,

and god piles on more shit than you can take.

the soaking wet sun throws a ray out from

behind a split black cloud, testing for protest.

I look for a rainbow, I

think there ought to be one,

and I can't say that it's not there, I

can only say that I don't see it.

THE OTHER WOMAN

when I learned I was

the other woman

my heart stopped.

briefly, I wondered how I would live on without it

as the blood drained from my face.

as the flood of shame, the ice of betrayal

overwhelmed me and brought me to my knees, I

felt my heart beat coming back but beating in a higher gear, racing to

the beat of drummers in a heavy metal band I did not hear,

shocking me,

rising up to such a scream I thought it might beat out of my chest,

and run across the floor in it's own dance without me.

days later,

utterly inept,

trembling with an awful awkwardness, nearing speechlessness,

I tried to explain to his wife that I was sorry,

so sorry,

I didn't know.

we sat at the kitchen table in their house,

it was covered with a red-white checkered cloth.

she made weak coffee I nearly spit out, struggling the find the needed words,

they were coming out in mumbling incompletes,

she watched my trembling and stopped it when she said,

"this is not your soap opera moment."

told me it had happened before,

I was not the first,

she was used to his endless infidelity,

it did not upset her any more.

shocked anew,

speechless twice,

I didn't understand,

those were sentences I had not expected.

how could she live with his lies?

I said I don't know why you stay with him, I did not expect her laugh.

her eyes were amused, her lips in a half-smile,

she said she stayed because she loved him,

and she stayed because he loved her,

and she stayed because of their small children

and she stayed because if she wanted to leave him—and she didn't—

where did I think she would go, with her family all in Charleston and

her friends with problems of her own?

and she stayed.

and she'd invited me to their house to see if I was really as naïve as

I had sounded when she called me, as naïve as he'd told her I was.

she handed me a cigarette, told me I was not like the others,

said,

you don't think like we do.

you think things are

black or white,

right or wrong,

lies or love,

good or bad.

we think of things that matter.

we hope we can pay the rent on time,

we hope we can fill the car with gas, enough to get to work and back,

we gotta hope we can pay the babysitter and still have money for food.

you worry about shit we never think about, things

that

DON'T

matter.

you stress about your homework,

how you gonna pay somebody else to cut your hair,

when you're gonna be able to get new clothes,

are you gonna be able to pass driver's ed.

I can't believe you need somebody to teach you that.

we just

get into the car

and **DRIVE.**

NICK

God had blessed this early April day with sun that danced on the river,

ducks that rode the water with their babies, small buds filled with promise

on slender branches gracefully swaying, encouraged by a gentle wind that

played with stands of my hair as I sat on the grasses, turned to watch Nick throw

small stones he'd gathered up to throw in the river, he laughed at the splashes,

each one made the river jump up in surprise.

stay on the grass, Nick. he said okay,

don't step in the mud, Nick. he said okay.

I smiled that he did not need as much as I did to make me happy,

I needed big things, he was happy with small stones he held in his upturned t- shirt.

I skipped a stone of my own across the river, just to see if it would make me laugh,

heard him cry out my name.

looked to see him sitting in the mud path,

sliding down to the liquid green of welcoming river,

oh my God no.

SAVE THE BOY!

within one heartbeat

I fell across the satanic mud path,

I was the log that stopped his feet I was the hand that pushed him up

I was the scream of fear I could not let him hear I was the voice that calmed him.

just move your feet, Nick. he said okay.

keep moving your feet, Nick, don't stop. he said okay.

I saw him up, up, up

there,

standing on the grass again,

a brown boy without stones,

without laughter.

what about you?

he cried out with a new fear,

and I saw where I was

and he saw where I was

and all of my thoughts froze my fingers jammed like spikes in the ground to hold me.

JUST DO THIS!
SAVE THE BOY!

save the boy stop his crying just inch up inch up.

when I felt the grasses I rolled when I felt the boy I hugged him I did not say a word.

ART ON THE WALL

my art hung on the far brick wall in the college town café where emeritus, alumni, students, civilians, staff sit at the tables on mismatched chairs grading papers, reading textbooks, taking notes, sipping hot breakfast crowd coffee.

my art.

on the wall.

when you came in, your jean jacket snapped all the way up to your chin, as if you feared a breath might escape, you sat away from me in a different booth, no hint of recognition as you walked right by me, your house has always reeked with the smell of cat piss, and that is why I never come there.

you have never been to this cafe.

how did you know about

my art on the wall?

I ordered a refill and the bread plate, waiting for Frank and my brother and his lover, Christine and Susan, we were all going to celebrate

my art on the wall.

I painted them chose them framed them named them, hung them up on hooks and nails left behind by other artists who's art hung on the wall.

there. is the one more realistic, (if you need reality painted), the ones inspired by the impressionists, the post impressionists, the cubists, the mannerists, that one, that portrait of the nude with her head on the footstool, that is the best I ever painted, it is not for sale.

I felt you in your jean jacket as a presence pushing into my back.

the morning sun forced it's rays through the window's panes without effort, touched the blues and yellows curiously, and then approved.

we left you there, I'd decided not to care about you at all. In the afternoon, Dick bought the painting of my seashells for two hundred dollars, when I picked up my check the next morning after I spilled hot coffee on my wrist, two men were standing there by "The Madonna", I hoped they would buy it, if they did, where would they hang it up when they got it home? and should I allow myself to feel proud of

my art on the wall.

even though you were no longer sitting in the booth of the day before, you might have been, so to hell with you and your always indifferent and easily given dismissal of all my pen and inks, charcoals, acrylics over all the years I knew you, as I cleaned my paint brushes in the kitchen sink while you judged the latest images I had formed, fought for. I felt the stabs of disappointment every time you said you did not like this one, did not like that one, and then you stopped coming to my house at all, did not return my cell phone calls, I imagined you filling the porch up with more stray cats, putting blankets and boxes out for them, and I never knew where you found all those goddamn boxes, I can't find any when I need one.

I let the cafe door swing shut behind me, it shrieked on old un-oiled hinges before it thumped against the wood of the door's frame, "The Madonna" was no longer there, the two men had bought and paid for

my art on the wall.

CHRISTMAS

Christmas comes way too often

even though it's only once each year.

I saw Christmas colored lights on three pine trees in someone's yard on Lake Street the week before Halloween and wished that I could stop my car, leave it running, run up, rip the strands of bulbs off, put up things that said "boo."

the last Christmas mom was alive it was 74 degrees and a way too sunny day, she cried because there was no snow, I cried because it was her last Christmas, and we all knew it just as well as she did, she bought us scarves and hats and gloves and mittens, she bought Dick a winter coat, she said she wanted us all to be warm after she was gone, she left us 6 months later on a night so heavy I did not wear the scarf she bought me for Christmas.

Tim said he was going to celebrate every Christmas after that better than he ever had before, his red pick-up slid and stuck in the mud farm in Streetsboro, he said he'd found the perfect tree to cut down for Christmas way back on someone's acreage, but there was no snow, the ground was not frozen, he walked all the way to the Twin Lakes bar to use the pay phone, call for a tow. I never knew how he got the truck to run after the mud bath, when I asked him he said he spent hours cleaning the mud from the front seats and steering wheel. he used to send us all poinsettias with detailed instructions on how to care for them so they would last all year, but mine always died, he sang along with the Grinch song he'd taped, and wanted me to sing, too.

I never did.

Tim died.

it's goddamn Christmas again,

it was just Christmas yesterday.

THE SOCIOPATH

she's too evil to walk upon the earth with people.

she never knocks,

she walks right in the front door, back door, breaks a window, there is nothing you can do to keep her out, she sets fire to everything you ever trusted in her, hides your mail, rips your clothes up, sets the thermostat to 75 and never pays the bill, what the hell, it's in your name. she erases your history.

she kills you. she loves the feel of death in her hands, she trembles with an ecstasy to watch the way it drips. drops on the kitchen floor you put down the new press and stick just last year.

she poisons with no pause, she shreds you up—it makes her dance— she rolls all the years you loved her around on her tongue until she's got them all, then spits them out with a force that burns you like an acid burns, eats, corrodes your spirit.

in the courtroom, you saw her, she takes out the sweetest smile from her left shirt pocket, plasters it on her face and the face of her current lover- witness- soon- to- be- next- casualty, she's so believably charming you just want to hold her close and rule in her favor.

I've seen you trying to wipe the shock off your eyes, but it won't come off, it's like the adhesive of industrial glue, and the god you pray to from your catholic religion is sociopathic, too, now the Christians won't like me, but it's the truth I know about, I've known the others just exactly like her, they are blue print rejects from hell.

I can see you dying from two hundred miles away.

I can send you jeans and cigarettes you can wear and smoke in your homelessness, but I can't pick you up, put your life together, and I can't feel your dreams die as well as you can, and I can't put a string of words together that will ever count as having mattered at all.

DEATH OF THE WIFE BEATER

spiders have woven a web in the corner of the ceiling closest to your bed, I noticed it this morning and thought it might be an omen, and it was.

I held your terrible hand until your brother left the room to get coffee in the cafeteria, then I dropped it, when it hit the sheets, it made a sound I didn't know existed.

that was my first act of defiance.

when you opened your eyes in protest, I bent low over your bed and damned you to hell.

they handed me your wedding ring, I had to take it, took it home and smashed it with your hammer on the concrete basement floor until it lay flat with no meaning, I gathered up and stuffed everything you ever owned or touched or wanted into big black lawn and leaf bags, drove all around town, throwing them in different dumpsters, would not donate to the Goodwill, no one should ever wear your clothes your shoes your shirts your leather jackets gloves full of fists I would never forget.

it will never be all right that you ripped my hope and innocence off me, a skin of me you held in your terrible hands for 7 years.

at the funeral your mother hugged me with whispered condolences, she assumed I was bereft, in need of comfort, I had to let her do it, say it, but I always thought she knew, how could she not know, she raised you, and your brother was your closest friend, what secrets did you share with him on those hunting trips and over way too many beers and shots of scotch at the sports bar?

at home.

alone.

the absences of loud and angry noises was my first joy.

I lit candles, put them in every room, and their flickering and cleansing flames blessed me.

RED LIGHT

this is a day I will smile at a memory,

even though the ground is dry and cracked and waiting for a rain.

my hands are dry and cracked like that when I finish scrubbing down the walls,

they wait for soothing lotion, like Cornhuskers.

I saw you in Wendy's yesterday, I did not stop to stare or dare to enter.

(god I hate those stained glass lamps they hang in every one of their restaurants, I used to repair them by the thousands in the stained glass shop I worked in, where Vince talked God talk every single day, he said he was going to convert me, that dripping Lutheran with his God song band).

I saw you stab your coke cup with your straw,

then looked away

quickly.

I walked on.

what would it be like not to be the overturned cart I saw on the sidewalk outside the grocery store parking lot, it's wheels up in the air helplessly, crying for someone to save it?

and wouldn't it be cool if you loved me?

I'd never stop at a red light again.

 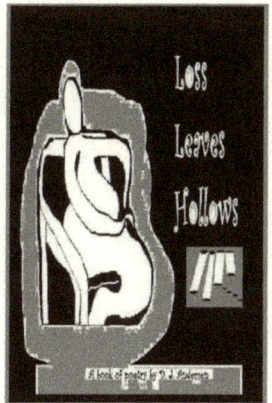 

Other books of Narrative Poetry by D. J. Andersen
For purchasing options, please visit our website:

www.BadgleyPublishingCompany.com

www.ingramcontent.com/pod-product-compliance
Lightning Source LLC
Chambersburg PA
CBHW051711040426
42446CB00008B/825